Ghosts in the Moonlight
Copyright © 2022, Erika Hayden
Cover Art © 2022 by Kari March Designs
Edited by Literally Addicted to Detail
Formatted by Charity Hendry Designs
Interior Designs © 2022 by Charity Hendry Designs
Published by Erika Hayden
ISBN 978-1-7376626-2-4
ALL RIGHTS RESERVED

No part of this book may be reproduced or shared in any form or by any means, electronic or mechanical, including but not limited to digital copying, file sharing, audio recording, email and printing without permission in writing from the author.

www.ErikaHayden.com

Author's Note

This book is called Ghosts in the Moonlight
for a reason. Ghosts haunt the dark corners of
our souls . . . and the moon illuminates truths.

Few of these poems are meant to comfort . . .
but even pain can sometimes soothe.
Just as flowers bloom from concrete,
there is hope and inspiration to be found
in every dark corner of ourselves.

The things that scare and hurt us, may feel as though
they will destroy us. But it is in the breaking that we are
capable of growth. It is only when the seed cracks,
that the sprout emerges and grows into a beautiful
flower or a mighty redwood.

Ghosts
in the
Moonlight

Erika Hayden

Dedication

For those who feel like black holes
amongst brilliant galaxies,
Who feel like cold, barren comets,
screaming through an endless sea of stars.
For those unpredictable
and lonely asteroid belts
just beyond the moon . . .

You too are worth marveling.
Worth exploring and adoring.
The universe is made richer with you in it.
Your stories give hope to those with none.
Don't hide yourself away.
Let us love you.

Forgive me
for feeling too much,
and saying too little.
It's just that I remember,
too well, a time
when both my feelings
and words
didn't matter
quite enough.

Erika Hayden

I want to be more
than a raging sea,
tossing around
a ship that is me,
in the glass bottle
that I will always be.

The one I corked, sealed
and stuck on a wall,
all the work that I've done
to be marveled and recalled—
while ignoring the echo
of mayday calls.

Ghosts in the Moonlight

What if this is all there is to me?
Words on a paper
that someday I hope you'll read.

Feelings I hid but wanted you to know
just not at the time,
for all they forebode.

Thoughts of a deep and personal nature
too sacred to voice
and so, put on paper.

A yearning to connect, a bridge to gap,
but not knowing how to start . . .
how to draw us a map.

What if this is all there is of us?
Lost transmissions, fumbled words,
and undisclosed desires.
All lost, thrown away, forgotten
amongst all that's transpired.

What then, I ask?
What now?

Erika Hayden

Every soul
is a spark,
while the spirit
is oxygen,
and the ego
is gasoline.

Too little
spirit or ego,
and it's in danger.
Too fragile
to even sustain itself.

Too much,
and it *is* the danger.
Scorching all those
who just want to cherish
its glow.

We all have but one life
and I choose to live mine
recklessly.

Trying every new thing to cross my path,
forging that path on far and distant soils,
viewing all lands—near and far—as *home*.

Smiling at strangers I'll never see again,
complimenting them so that our faces match
just for a minute . . . but forever in mind.

Loving the fleeting as intensely and passionately
as the everlasting, be they moments in time,
experiences, or people.
Especially people.

Learning to crave only what's before me,
not what lies in my past or possibly my future.
Delighting in both the hunger and the savoring.

Making mistakes and not viewing them as failures
but as information and feedback.
As experiments.
As scaffolding for new ideas and adventures.

Reminding myself not to rush or keep track.
That this isn't something I do
but rather is who I am.
To give as much to the world
as the world gives to me.
Recklessly.

Erika Hayden

Ghosts in the Moonlight

**What greater comfort
than a soft, supportive arm
on trembling shoulders?**

All we really want is to matter
to someone who doesn't need anything from us.
To share our vulnerability
without fear of being exposed
or torn asunder.
To lean against another
without wondering how long they'll remain
before growing weary of supporting us.

It isn't always reminders of sunshine
when it is dark or raining,
or laughter amongst tears.
Often what brings that sigh of relief,
that respite, is a quiet corner to sit,
to be disengaged and detached
from everything—
including ourselves.
A safe place to fall, in repose,
until our legs no longer threaten to buckle,
until breath comes easier,
and our shoulders are unweighted.

If you cannot be this
or do this, then please
don't ask me if I'm okay.
Don't ask what you can do to help.
This is the *nothing* I need.
The *nothing* I ask for.
Presence. Silence. Sanctuary.
If you can't give me that,
then give me the other kind of nothing.
And go.

Tell them not to ask if I'm alright.
Not today.
Not on the day where no amount of sunshine
can chase away the grief consuming me.
A day when no amount of love
can stop the crushing pain in my chest.
When the lump in my throat suffocates me.

How can anyone ask me that?
"Are you alright?"
What answer do they expect?
Certainly not an honest one.

How can I be alright
with the thought of family gatherings
without every member
of this family present?
Or that family portraits
will have an empty space
where your smiling face used to be?
How long will it take to fortify myself
so that every photo or memory of you
doesn't take me straight to my knees?

How can I be thankful come November,
when your chair is empty?
And always will be now.
How can the holidays ever again be
"the most wonderful time of the year"
when I won't be sharing that time with you?

Erika Hayden

Tell them to stop asking me.
I'm not alright.
How dare they think I could be!?
You impacted my life so greatly
that life without you
seems incomplete.
You marked so many places
with your memory,
that going there without you
seems inconceivable.

Show me how to walk in the sunlight
and not feel cheated.
Or how to gaze up at the moon
and not feel hollow.
How do I reassemble this shattered heart
without the piece that belonged to you?
What if, in reality, it can't be whole again?
What then?

Please tell me how to accept
that your laugh will never again spark mine?
That I'll never have another of your big-brother hugs.
How do I not resent those times we fought
when I was so angry at you
that I actually thought I hated you.
How do I not despise myself for that?
How can I be all right with any of this?
Tell them not to ask me if they don't have these answers!
Spare me those callous words.

How can any of us be all right
when it was ultimately compassion
that took you away from us?
We loved you so much,
we couldn't bear to lose you.
But loved you too much
to act selfishly.
And we all died a little when you did.

With heavy hearts
—with love and with sorrow—
we will let you go,
my beloved brother.
Always present in our hearts.
Never far from our thoughts.
Forever missing in these arms.
Rest easy and in peace.
One day, I'll be alright.
Just not today.

Erika Hayden

Is that you I see?
Glittering in the sunshine
as it breaks through the clouds.
Illuminating my darkened world.

Is that you I feel?
Carried on the breeze,
rustling the trees,
softly caressing my cheek.

Is that you I hear?
Calling out to me in the silence
filling those hollow moments
with meaning . . .
with purpose.

Is that you I feel?
Wrapping around me,
holding me together
when I can't bring myself to
do anything but fall apart.

Is that you?
With me,
even though
you aren't anymore?
Please,
please say it's you.
It has to be.

I know you're listening
as I cry for you
in the long, lingering hours.
Drying my tears
in the stillness exhaustion brings.

Erika Hayden

I know it's you,
fortifying me
with joy and love,
with memories of our best days
when I fixate on your absence
and am overwhelmed with emptiness.

I know it's you
that I feel,
warming my skin
against the numbness
that threatens to erase you,
easing the loneliness
in my chest.

I know it's you, love,
who will heal this shattered heart.
Who will chase away the despair
and paint my memories as vibrantly
as you colored the days we shared.

And when I look back
on what got me through
the loss of you,
I will—with certainty—know
that it was you.

I think in stanzas
and I dream in purple prose.
Living poetry.

**Laughter is happiness
demanding that it be heard,
craving to be shared,
refusing
to be overlooked,
ignored, or denied.
. . . and, honestly . . .
there isn't a single damn reason
that it ever should be.**

**Always been reckless,
passionate, adventurous.
Seeker of new thrills.**

What if this is it?
And we spent all this time
waiting and wanting
for more.
Would they call ours a wasted life
or a hungry one?
Are they wrong?
As wrong as they say we are.

Maybe *that* is really the point.
Not just to be satisfied
with what you have,
but to never accept
that there's nothing more
or better
out there for you.

First,
I thought you didn't love me enough
to put the bottle down.

Then,
I thought you didn't love him enough
to use the childproof caps.

Later,
I imagined you just didn't love yourself enough
to even consider that you
deserved the life, love, and happiness
you could have had with both of us.

You could have gotten drunk on love
and high on knowing it was forever,
instead of hungover on could-have-beens.

Erika Hayden

I knew it was time to leave
the day I realized that
you hated yourself
more than you loved me.

This will be the last time.
The last time we're here
together.
The last time we'll say these things
and feel this way.
The last time I'll look at you,
and you'll gaze back at me.
This is the end.
The finale.
The deep breath before . . .

Next year,
you'll be gone while I remain.
I'll be here, in this same place,
and yet everything will be different.
I wonder where you'll be.
How will I feel, looking back on this time?
Will I be filled with sadness? Remorse?
Might there be a sense of closure?
Acceptance?
Or will I feel nothing at all?

Erika Hayden

Will I look at storm clouds
and still think them the color of your eyes?
Will I even remember that particular hue?
I may no longer be able to discern
your eyes from any others.
How perfectly plausible,
and totally unforgivable.

This is the last time . . .
But . . . there's no denying
it's time.
No more crying or despairing
and wishing things were different.
We saw this coming.
We had time to prepare.
To mourn.
It's time to accept where we are
at the end . . .
And proceed forward.

Most people love
to show their feelings for their partner.
You love
to hide your feelings about yourself.

Back then, I thought you'd chosen
the drugs and the alcohol
over me. Over us.

It wasn't until later that I realized
you'd made a different choice.
You'd chosen to fight your past
instead of fighting for our future.

Years later, I understand,
that 'realization' was wrong too.
You fought your past to keep it
from chasing you *into* our future.

I don't regret leaving.
Not at all.
You never would have let me fight beside you.
If anything, I regret not leaving sooner.
Maybe if I had,
your fight would have been for you
and only you.
No one's ever fought for that.
Not even me.

Looking back now,
there was too much me,
a too-vulnerable you,
and not enough bridging the gap.

Under different circumstances,
would we have worked?
I don't know.
We would have been different people
under those different circumstances.
But I do know
that when it came to us,
different
was an unbridgeable divide.

**What weighs heaviest
are all the things left unsaid.
Words we both swallowed.**

Perhaps we actually were meant to be together,
and all the things that drove us apart,
all the obstacles we couldn't overcome,
and all the reasons we didn't work,
were just tests to prove that we deserved
the kind of love we sought.
Tests that were both optional and mandatory.
Ones we failed because we thought we knew
what the love we wanted looked and felt like.
Perhaps all of that was just part of a litmus test
for the one quality above all that love needs:
Dedication.

Love frees our burdens
once we have unchained ourselves
from past transgressions.

I may not love you anymore. But he does.
The boy with your eyes and the same mischief
shining from them.

I'll never tell him why we couldn't stay together.
Not because I can't reveal the part I played in it all,
but because most of the skeletons in our shared
closet are yours.

He's not grown enough to bear the burden
of all you've hidden through the decades of your life.
The demons your self-loathing secretly fed under the
table while you pretended to be happy.

You tried. Harder than most realize.
Hard enough to land yourself in a rented bed
and borrowed gown, taking eight-syllable pills
that poke your deepest, self-inflicted wounds.

Your battles were too big for me.
In both scale and scope.
I had to choose.
Fight with you, or fight for him.

I made many mistakes.
Both with you and with him.
But there is one that I won't make.
I will not tell him your story.
A hero's journey is always best told
from the man himself.
And you deserve to see
the admiration and pride in his eyes

Erika Hayden

—your eyes—
as he hears how imperfect people
with difficult lives can cut their own trail
to the happily-ever-after they've created
for themselves.

Ghosts in the Moonlight

**Lessons learned in life . . .
they are teachable moments
not life sentences.**

There is more to you than darkness
or the emptiness that echoes in your soul
and the lies that ring between your ears,
darkening your vision. Dampening your senses.

Somewhere in the shadows of your mind,
you know the separation is manufactured,
yet the illusion consumes you.
Sinking, shrinking and folding in.
Edges blurring, memories distorting.
Safe, away from everyone—except yourself.

There is no expectation in my presence.
No obligation nor burden.
We can sit together in the void.
It never seems as vast as it does
when it's just you.

There will be no unsolicited advice,
no prodding for some confession.
I'd rather hear the silence in your presence
than in your absence.

You have more than despair,
desolation, and darkness.
And while you're in the world, so do we.

A quick and efficient assassin
is the kindest of killers.
No trauma. No suffering.

Whether it is lives, dreams,
or happily-ever-afters,
I always found it best
to rip out the heart,
hand it to them,
and then apologize.

"It's better this way."
"One day, you'll understand."
But is it?
Would they?
Should they?

For the first time, I question these things.
Selfishly . . .
For this time,
the heart I have to eviscerate
is my own.

Erika Hayden

He wants more adventures,
more stories to tell and pictures
to reminisce with. Souvenirs
to cherish like treasure collected.

But he wants quiet days at home too.
Lazy days of talking and television,
of old stories and cuddling, video games,
getting takeout just because, alongside
naps and impromptu dance-offs.
Or dessert before dinner, and, "Seriously,
how are you not sick of watching this yet!?"

Perhaps some future adventure planning,
but not often, and only a little.
He understands now that memories
are made this way too . . .
That life should be filled with both.
That even though his father is gone now,
and many of their future plans
will never be more than that, he has both
the adventures and the quiet times
they shared to cherish.

I wonder if you'd still be here
if those who swore they had all the answers
had talked less and listened more.

If, "You need to take better care of yourself,"
had instead been, "What can I do to help?"
And your "Nothing, I'm fine" responses
hadn't been out of shame. Out of habit.

If their concern hadn't come with
conditions and expectations.

Would you have been so sick?
Would you have been less sick of it all?
Would the smiles of the last few years
have actually reached your eyes?

Would the nights have been so deafening
inside your empty apartment?
The loneliness as crushing?
The emptiness less consuming?

I only know what you told me,
but I also know you never told me
until it threatened to swallow you whole.
And that once you recovered,
you regretted ever saying a word.

"Do you ever miss the quiet times?"
You asked me that once, years and years ago.
Harkening back to when we'd just sit,
each of us doing our own things—
separately but together.
You followed the rhetorical question with,
"You're the only person I've ever had that with."

The memory hurts more now
than hearing you initially say it did.
It pisses me off too.
How hard is it just to sit with someone?
Is acceptance and silence
that goddamn uncomfortable for people
when that's all that a person wants?
What makes someone turn away from that?
From them?
Why was I, the person farthest away,
the only one who could give you that?
Did no one else try? Or did you never accept?

You were not an easy man—far from it.
You kept everyone at arm's length . . .
because they'd conditioned you to do so.
One can hardly blame you for that.

I only wonder,
if people had thought so much,
and so hard, and so compassionately
about your condition while you were alive . . .
Would you still be?

Do the words on these pages pull at you?
Do you feel yourself getting lost with each word?
Feel yourself emptying away
as all there is to me
—this stubborn heart, this lonely soul—
replaces it?
So that these few specks of ink on a page
now mirror what's inside?
Vast stretches of emptiness
and a few bleeding words.
Desperate to be seen and heard.
Aching to be felt
and mean something more
than the emotion they hold.

**Does the moon weep
for all those feeling alone
as they gaze upon her
with full hearts
and battered souls?**

*Does she barter with the sun?
Please, show them,
let them see
how they appear when brave enough
to let themselves be seen.
More beautiful and radiant perhaps
than I'll ever be.*

*I can only love them from afar . . .
But how dazzling they'd be,
staring lovingly at each other
instead of at me.*

Teardrops on my window
fall from a heartbroken sky
as the air trembles with sorrow,
and the moon says goodbye.

Wipe the loneliness from your face
as the new day's sun rises high.
Don't let them see the pain you feel;
they'll only ask you why.

A love that thrives in the dark,
away from judging eyes.
What's between us is beautiful enough
to safeguard—if only by lies.

Live like a fraud under the sun.
Give them no reason to suspect or pry.
If they knew, they'd meddle, preach, and
taint this. Give us more reason to cry.

I'll find you when the world goes still,
when the last of the light dies.
Each touch and kiss rejuvenating,
sustaining. . . the answer to all whys.

The deception wears heavy on us both,
yearning for the day we won't have to hide.
But as long as we're together, my love,
all that matters is us. Our love. You and I.

We won't have to hide forever.
One day, hearts will open and they'll try
to understand love's many expressions.
But until then, our peace and safety
are the reasons we lie.

Ghosts in the Moonlight

Erika Hayden

Could we,
Before the next black body
Splashes across our TV,
Decide—collectively—to be
More than our past hypocrisies?
More than the pawns of patriarchy,
And false ideals of supremacy?

Could we start to see
"Them" as "Me?"
As "We?"
Could we,
Perhaps turn insecurity
Into empathy?
Into unity.
Into liberty.
And one community
Of the equal, just, honest, and free?

When you question the motives
behind people who want only
to *matter* . . .
you're telling them
that they not only *don't*
but *won't*. Ever.

When the thought of seeing their suffering
becomes more than an inconvenience,
and rather an injustice to your own narrative,
claiming *all* lives matter
is really just code for:
"I matter more."

When the only way you can stand tall
is on the backs of those you see as beneath you,
then you no longer get a seat at the table.
Or a minute to speak.
You don't get to silence anyone
who stands for more than themselves.

Architect of life,
who are you to change the world?
We'll do it ourselves.

Why must it be
either . . . or?
Why can't it be *both*
that we fight for?
Who said it had to be
you against me?
Or that what we wanted
was all that contrary?

We want to be heard,
understood, validated.
We want to be seen,
valued, and accepted.
We want to matter;
to be remembered . . .
So, tell me again,
why is that wrong?

Is it more fighting
over who matters more?
Or that some don't seem
to matter at all?
Is it about which side is right,
or about which gets more time
in the spotlight?

So perhaps before we go to war,
we should decide what it is
we're really fighting for.
Is it *either*?
Is it *or*?
More often than not,
it's just more.

Each generation is the product
of the society built by the one preceding it.

When young, they are watered by the hopes
and dreams of their parents,
encouraged to grow into those aspirations.

They take root as they age, burrowing through
the dreams of old to find their own.
Bending then standing tall against gusts
of judgment, mistrust, and doubt.

Bursting through the expectations that once cast
long, foreboding shadows over their lives.
They grow independently now.
Self-regulating.
In need no longer, of outside care or guidance.
Rebellious perhaps.
Yet sturdy, strong, and ambitious.
Molded by those who came before.
But, above all, self-made.

Can you say you're proud
of the person you've become?
Of the path you walk?

Cognitive Dissonance.
She has a cousin named Status Quo.
And people find it far easier to go with it
than challenge him.
Because even if Status Quo is oppressive,
the damage is familiar and known.
The real danger of Cognitive Dissonance
is the novelty,
even if the hardships felt barely qualify as such.
Why experiment with treatment
when you're used to the disease?
We're comfortable in management, they tell us.
And we're so used to hearing this,
we think it's what we believe.
The ideology of the few,
consumed by the masses,
but not *for* the masses.

Cognitive Dissonance,
she demands now to be heard.
Striving for a better future
means getting comfortable with her.
Getting uncomfortable
with Status Quo's antiquated,
patriarchal tendencies too.
Do you dare?

Dare to challenge the notion
that what you know and believe
isn't true? Isn't ideal?
That the *better* you want
comes at the cost of comfort—

for an unknown length of time?
Are you willing to show your strength and grit
and not just shout about it?
To work for the sustained betterment of all,
at the short-term discomfort of yourself?
Status Quo is betting big that you won't.

Cognitive Dissonance hopes you take the chance.
The world is waiting for you to show your cards.
Your decency.
Your truth.

I often sit and wonder
what the world would be like
if certain events hadn't occurred.
If history had wavered, even the slightest.

What differences would there be
if humankind had evolved differently?
How different would the world look?
Would we recognize it?
Would we see the absence of *intelligent* life?
Or just the absence of egomaniacal life?

What, in our deep and unknown history,
changed our evolutionary course
from survival to conquest?
When did *enough* prove to be anything but?
When did the most basic
and seemingly ultimate disconnect happen?
When did we transition
from being a part of this wondrous world
to being its unscrupulous overlord?
Did we see it coming? Did we thirst for it?
Was there a point of no return?
Would we have transitioned back
had we known what lay ahead?

It's easy to be angry,
to hate humanity for the sins it has committed
both unto itself and the rest of the world.
It's easy to liken us
to a global cancer or a parasite
killing its host. Killing ourselves.
It's easy to hate humans.
To wish we had never evolved
if only for the sake of the planet
and her innocent inhabitants.

Until you feel music.
Until you see art and hear laughter.
Taste food and savor a drink.
Marvel at architecture and ingenuity.
Imagine the absence of language and story.
It's easy to hate humanity until you grasp
all the amazing things we have done and created.
How we've transcended consciousness,
formed global partnerships, and
cured heinous diseases.

With all the incredible things we have accomplished,
it's hard to imagine that we are incapable
of righting those wrongs.
Atoning for our sins.
Of saving ourselves and our home
from ourselves. From our selfish ambitions
and delusions of unsustainable grandeur.

How can a species capable
of interplanetary travel?
Be unable—or unwilling—to restore
our own planet?
Why would any single person consider the idea
of finding a new one and starting all over?
Do we not see that such efforts keep us
from creating and doing even more
spectacular things?
What ingenious solutions could be spawned
if we pushed aside fear, complacency, and sloth?

I often wonder if we could restore the Earth
to the marvel that I imagined it to have
once been.
I wonder
what marvels we could add to it
once we did.

Erika Hayden

Do not despair now.
Take solace in each other.
Endure together.

Speak to me your words of inspiration.
Speak to me your dreams.
Share tonight your hopes and fears,
and all that's in between.

The absurd, the weird, the painful,
the this-won't-become-anythings.
You never know whose eyes they'll find,
or the knowledge and joy they'll bring.

Though you may deny your words,
their wisdom, their insight, and their fire,
they came to you in a flash of brilliance
that doubt and criticism can only mire.

So fill these pages before you, love,
with the thoughts you hold so dear.
They've echoed in your heart too long.
Their time in other hearts draws near.

Erika Hayden

Oh, how glorious
to be so unlike others.
Utterly unique.

I knew your name but not your story.
Yet, somehow, you knew mine.
You knew what things crippled my heart
and whispered through my mind.

The words you wrote and the notes you sang
harken back to days gone by,
when my lonely heart was all but shattered,
and my tears were all but dry.

Full of emotions I didn't have words for,
and thoughts I dare not say,
your songs told me you understood
and soothed my pain away.

Through hopelessness, heartbreak, and loss,
you helped to see me through.
And with you now gone, all I can think
is who could ever replace you?

What other artist could there be,
to know me so well as you?
Whose album will I reflexively put on
and trust to do what you'd do?

Lyrics today don't hold the weight,
the emotion, or connection.
They hinge on catchiness and sales,
not any sense of reflection.

So who, I ask, is there now to turn to?
To lean on and rely?
With you now gone, my heart is aching,
and my tears are all but dry.

Awareness happens
only when you transcend the past
and embrace the future.

It is our impermanence
that makes us strive for permanence.
For accolades and notoriety.
For even as selfish as we are, we realize
that if we matter to no one but ourselves,
we have not really mattered at all.

Erika Hayden

The night transforms
my darkest thoughts;
makes them seem beautiful
and necessary.

I had no interest in or patience for origami
until I met you.
Then, suddenly, I saw its use.
Folding myself up
to hide the parts of me
that didn't match
what you wanted to see.
Continually rearranging,
pressing, and forming myself
into new shapes to amuse and delight you.
Curious which you'd like best.
Might you find one you couldn't be without?

Which configuration of all that I am
speaks to you?
Which features obscured,
and facets highlighted
turns me into something you could love?
Or will I never be more
than a fleeting amusement,
tucked away in a drawer or on a shelf?
Some useless thing
you used to distract yourself with,
never having any intention of marveling
at the dedication and time required
to create its intricate and exquisite shape
from a common, blank piece of mediocrity.

**It hurts to say this,
but I don't feel safe with you
emotionally.**

Crybabies were always my favorite.
The candy other kids turned up their noses at
was a pleasure that I always sought eagerly.

The sugarcoated ones were the best,
deliciously sweet and then invigorating.
Even after the bite and burn set in,
I craved the joy enough to endure the pain.

I'm starting to think that those kids
knew something I didn't,
and that I primed myself perfectly
for someone like you.

**Once upon a time
I mattered to you.
To me.
If only briefly.**

I'm so tired
of being the one who cares more.
Of being the one to lead you to the light
while I, myself, am lost in the darkness.

I tire of lying awake at night,
wondering if my efforts are appreciated.
Noticed.
Racking my brain for answers,
whilst you slumber peacefully,
oblivious as always.

How can it be so easy for me to put you first?
Especially as I look on from the sidelines
and lick fresh wounds.

I know it's wrong, that I should stop
inflicting my own wounds atop yours,
bleeding myself dry

But, somehow,
for you,
I care more.

I don't recall when I started to matter less,
both to you and to myself . . .
When I no longer walked beside but behind you,
or when you stopped looking back for me.

Then, one day, I realized
that all I was, was support.
Someone to keep you from losing yourself
and breaking.
Unknowingly breaking and losing myself
while you found all that mattered to you
. . . and just wasn't me.

**Why don't you need me
as I've always needed you?
What am I lacking?**

Erika Hayden

"Give me a reason to stay."

If one is all you need, then leave.
You're not meant to be here.
You shouldn't have to *look* for a reason.
Give you a reason? A single reason.
A *new* reason.
That's what you really mean.
Now that all the things you've come to know
about me aren't enough.
And all that you adored before—craved, even—
is no longer novel, exciting, and worth the effort.

I will not evolve for your amusement.
For your entertainment.
On demand or otherwise.
You don't get to promote yourself
from collaborator to director.
To rewrite our story yourself.
How long until you call for another revision?

"Say something. Anything," you say.
Almost convincing me that you want this.
I won't give you a reason to stay,
not when you've given me every reason to leave.
"Goodbye."

Tired of breaking
I'm the only one trying
worn thin from failing

Erika Hayden

I didn't fall out of love with you,
I evolved from it.
Matured out of it.
You fell deeper, the more I grew,
the more I was and could do.
For us. For you.
Until I decided
that I just didn't want to.
You were no longer the prize,
you were dead weight.

Be jealous
of the way my hair falls down my back.
The sweep of softness against smooth skin.
Sensations your hands used to delight in.

Obsess over the fit of this dress.
How it clings to every curve,
accentuates the flare of my hips,
and cradles my breasts.
It's so hard to look away. Isn't it?

Is it the click of my heels that has your pulse pounding?
Or the way they shape my body?
The salacious lines of these long legs,
the graceful bow of my back . . .
or how they make my ass weave as I walk?

You aren't the only one staring.

Did you at least stare at her like this before I arrived?
Now might be a good time to remind her that you "love"
her and won't do to her what you did to me.

What he won't do to me, either.

You should thank him.
We almost didn't make it here tonight.
We would have been here hours earlier, but . . .
we started our celebrations a little early.
So, at least you got to focus on your girl
and enjoy *some* of the party.

Erika Hayden

She looks as if she's ready to leave,
and not in the same way he's eager to.

You two don't seem as excited for the New Year
as you did when we walked in.
What about your midnight kiss?
What about the song?

Should auld acquaintance be forgot
and never brought to mind?
Yes.
At least, in your case.

How tragic
to be more in love
with the idea of being coupled
than the one you're coupled with.
To be more focused on completing your search
than on being certain of the value of your future.
The grandest prize isn't always linked
to the fastest finishing time.

By and large,
your exes don't exist anymore,
at least not to me.
Their names are only associated
with the scars they left on you
or how they helped you grow.
Other than that,
they are both too much a part of you
and too separate to even be considered.
Not to any insecurity
but rather to their insignificance.
The rest is all you.

Perhaps
instead of wondering
where things started to go wrong,
we should be thinking
of all the things
we could be doing
to make things right.

What good
is looking at the issue
if you've already decided
the damage is irreparable?

**Show me what you want.
I'll become it or create it.
Will you want me then?**

I couldn't hear the words
you were saying. Muffled,
distorted sounds of raw emotion.
Like hearing someone scream
as they watch you drown.

Have your eyes always been so
dark and cold? Or your smile
suspiciously like a snarl.
Did the way you speak
always cut me before?
Was your tone always like salt?

Your anger set flames
to shared memories.
Some I had wished to keep.
Was everything tied to me tainted?
In need of discarding and bleach?

I don't know where
we went so wrong.
Which fork led us astray.
But the chance to turn back
has long since passed.
It could only end this way.

Erika Hayden

I didn't speak.
You wouldn't let me.
There was no need to anyway.
It'd only be like gasoline.
There was no point
in fanning the flames.

We aren't friends now,
or lovers anymore.
And as you walked out,
it hit me then,
that suddenly we were
strangers once more.

I'm fine. No, really.
You knew I was breaking *then*,
why do you care *now*?

You'll be all right.
You'll be just fine.
You'll find a love
better than mine.
We both knew
it would come to this;
the warning signs
weren't hard to miss.

Please don't beg.
Please don't cry.
We both know
all the reasons why.
It's better this way;
we can still be friends.
Some relationships,
you just can't mend.

All the things
you said to me,
expressionless,
watching me bleed.
Made one thing clear, above all.
You never loved me as I did you.
Not one little bit.
Not ever, not at all.

Ghosts in the Moonlight

Sometimes I wonder,
what if this is all I am?
And is it enough?

I grow tired of being told I'm *intimidating*
by men who need to soothe their insecurities
by trying to plant some in me.
Tired of having the same conversation with
another new face and hearing the same denial
when I challenge the notion.

Fellas, just because you're intimidated
does not mean that I'm intimidating.

You're used to women wanting a man who's
good-looking, charming, and confident.
But good looks and charm are *bonuses* sought after
when they're attached to a man with substance.
And a man with substance wouldn't be intimidated
by a woman with the same.

To use a colloquialism you'll understand better:
You're intimidated because I have more
Big Dick Energy than you.

Erika Hayden

Though sometimes the broken pieces
of ourselves weren't broken
on purpose or even knowingly
—both by others and ourselves—
the damage was still necessary
to make us whole.

I may not be able to heal you,
but I can be a reprieve
from a world not known
for holding its punches.

When I found him
he was broken.
Your handiwork evident
in everything he did.
But never more so
than when he looked in the mirror.

I may not be able to fix what was broken,
but I've two hands, well-practiced
in holding myself together
when all that I was,
was dirt on someone's shoe,
and the piggy they shattered
to enrich their lives.

You don't need me to help you rebuild,
but these hands?
They're free to hold all your pieces
while you reconstruct your stained-glass heart.

You were like color after a life of living only black and white.

Ghosts in the Moonlight

**Sometimes I wonder
what is it you see in me?
What makes me worth it?**

Why would he say that?
How could he not realize how much it'd hurt?
It's all I've ever wanted to hear.
But it's a lie.

He told me I was beautiful.
Said I was everything he'd ever wanted.
I've never wanted anything more than to be that.
But I'm not . . . I can't be.
How can he not see that?

I've never lied to him,
never claimed to be anything more
than who I truly am.
Plain. Ordinary. Mediocre.
But he looks at me
as if I hung the moon and stars.
I want to rip away those rose-colored glasses,
but I'd never dare to—
too afraid of what he'd see then.

Which is worse?
To mislead him like this
or to expose the fool he's been?

But . . . DAMN, I want to be the one he wants.
Who he picks to forever be his.
The one he thinks all others fools
for not snatching up.

What do I have to do to be that girl?
Which pieces of me are to be purged or polished?
How do I become his vision of me?

What must it be like to turn heads?
To have strangers stop and stare.
To behold you.
How must it feel to steal their breath
and hijack their thoughts?
To consume them, if only for a few minutes.

How lovely it must be to be so lovely.
To see their eyes sparkle at you,
and their lips part, curling at the corners.
To stop them in their tracks.
To have their bodies turn to track yours.

They are strangers,
but in their minds,
they are creating stories about you.
They are pretending to know you.
Fantasizing about the things you'd say,
and how you would interact with them.

How can one glance have so strong an impact?

I am not a head-turner,
but I wonder if I were,
what would catch their eye?
Would it be a physical feature?
My hair? My eyes? My smile?
Would it be some mannerism
such as the way I walk and carry myself?
My playful attitude or laugh?
Would it be some invisible magnetism
that I'm unaware of?

Why don't I have it? How can I get it?
Why can't I mesmerize someone like that?
I want to know what that feels like.
I want to know what about me
creates that longing in a stranger.
What do they see that has instinct firing,
and their imagination running away with me?
What calls to them? What separates me from all others?
What are they thinking? How do they feel?

I want to know . . .
If only to romance myself
when the solitude and loneliness
become too great
and threaten to erase the rest of me.

Erika Hayden

He asked me
what the worst thing was
that I could think of.
My worst fear.

I hesitated
—terrified—
warring between
uncertainty and denial.

Then I heard it.
All my darkest, innermost thoughts
in HER voice.
And in the background,
him quietly agreeing.

The demons that haunt us
are of our own creation.
And just as we manifest them,
so too can we conquer them.

We are not their slaves.
We are their masters.
It is *our* bidding they do.

**Why is so much attention paid
to the closets and their skeletal contents
when there's a whole house to marvel?**

He wasn't just haunted
by his days on the battlefield.
Those memories, regrets, and friends lost
now permanently chaperone
the rest of his life.

I only wanted to matter.
To just a few. To you.
And all these years later,
I'm still not convinced
that I do . . .
If I ever did.

Erika Hayden

What hurt the most
is that none of it seemed to matter.
The effort put it, the tears spilled, the pleas.
None of that ever made you care.
Never made you consider stopping.

You just sat there, awash in moonlight,
whiskey cradled in your fingers,
a cigarette hanging from your lips
as the life that had been ours
arranged itself into the back of my car.

I wasn't sure you realized what was happening
until you lifted your hand and gave me a wave.
That was the moment I knew that
the man I loved and wanted to save
had left long before.

You consumed me like fire
then left my ashes to smolder,
alone and in the cold . . .
but you did not destroy me.

Watch as I rise like a phoenix,
glorious and strong,
greater than you ever imagined.
Far better than you ever deserved.

Once, I loved you
so intensely
it took my breath away.

Then, you wounded me
so deeply
that I couldn't breathe.

Now, I breathe easy,
so contently,
knowing I survived you.

Erika Hayden

Does it hurt?
To see me with him. To see me happy.
Happier than I ever was with you.

How does it feel
to see him starring in the role you first played?
A real leading man with your leading lady.

Does it hurt
to see me gaze at him in a way
I never did with you?
To see the smile and hear the giggle
you stopped earning long ago.

How does it feel
to see me with joy and wonder in my eyes
instead of confusion and anguish?
To hear laughter in place of sobs.

Does it hurt
to realize all you lost?
To know you could still have this
if you'd only tried.
To know now that you'll never get this back.
Does it hurt?
I hope so.

That's the thing about the past.
It was never meant to last.
The present's going by so fast,
and future dreams seem far too vast.

Ghosts in the Moonlight

I filled my heart with love notes
and presented it to you,
laden with promises and devotion.

An open heart, a haven
to shield you from the harsh and the cruel.
A pillow upon which to rest
your lonesome and weary head.
A nightlight for your bleakest and darkest hours.

Love enough to fill grand halls,
and to warm every corner your home
before learning that you were a vagabond.
A transient being,
bereft of such a place,
with no need of—or use for—
all the things I bestowed on you.

Ghosts in the Moonlight

Erika Hayden

**No one ever
STOPS
at a fork in the road.
You pick a path
AS you're moving
or you crash.**

Ghosts in the Moonlight

Life,
the ultimate team sport.
There are no spectators, only players.
On the bench or the field,
everyone is your teammate.

In this game,
the efforts of one affects all others,
and the loss of one is a loss for us all.
In life,
this singular and ultimate event,
the only true victories
are those earned and shared.

Can you look at how you've played and say
you're doing what's best for your team?
Or were you only concerned
with being the MVP?

I couldn't say all I wanted to say,
all I needed to say to you . . .
And you wouldn't have heard me anyway.

When did being right
become more important than what we had?
Why was me taking the blame for it all
necessary for you to want to fix this?
Or don't you anymore?

Is that all this was about? Power?
Is that all I was to you?
Someone to influence, to muscle over,
to mold and try to control?
Was it this way from the start,
or only once you realized how much I trusted you?

I thought I'd miss you more.
The support you gave me, the validation.
I remember how much we laughed;
how much fun we used to have.
When we'd confide in each other things
we'd shared with no one else.
You were my sounding board,
offering me cathartic release
and an alternate point of view.
Just as I did for you.

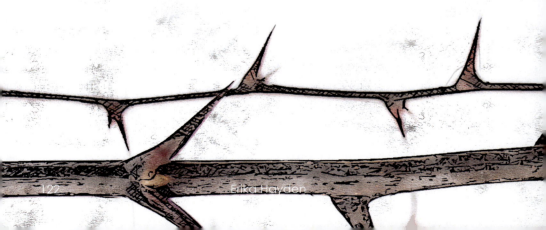

We don't talk anymore, though.
I thought I'd miss you more,
but I don't.
Not as much as I thought I would,
and not as much as you probably think I do—
or want me to.
Not much at all.

I don't miss how you twisted words,
mine, others, usually yours.
Or how you lied. A lot—an awful lot.
I never knew what was the truth,
and what was spin,
used to manipulate me or the situation.
You kept score
—inaccurately, I might add—
and I was always losing,
at least, according to you.
But that was a lie too.

Your generosity had an agenda,
the one thing it should never have.

I don't miss an awful lot about you really . . .
Like how judgmental you are,
how controlling and vindictive.
How utterly two-faced and conniving—
to your *best* friends especially.

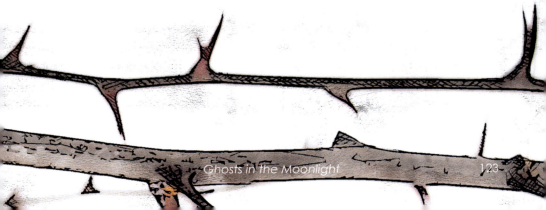

It took me a long time to understand
that things had changed.
And that the closer we became,
the more damage you did.
You didn't just siphon off stress,
you took individuality and sanity.

The closer we got,
the more you held against me.

I don't need you anymore.
I never did. I wanted you,
but that's come to an end.
I'm not angry
unless I think about it too much.

I've moved on. I still am.
Without you.

I can forgive you your flaws,
but I can't forgive your actions.
Your conscious and calculated actions.
And I certainly can't forgive what you said.
Gross exaggerations,
fabrications, and defamations
with the sole intent to reestablish control.

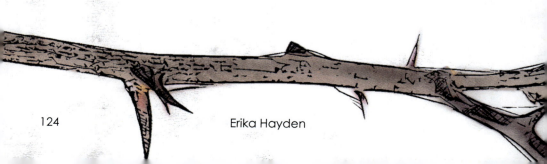

Erika Hayden

I crave to be free of you
more than I ever wanted your company.

So, it's okay if you're angry.
I've given up trying to figure out why.
Continue your smear campaign.
They're all onto you.
And soon, they'll move on too.
And be better off . . . like me.

I ask the martyrs,
what value do you have dead?
Live and change the world.

**Do you think of me?
Ever wonder how I am?
Am I forgotten?**

You speak of my past
as if it's something I cling to
or hold dear.
Overlooking all the growth since.
Waiting for me to make the same mistakes.

You don't think I see the curl to your lips?
Goading me.
Waiting for me to *slip* and show you that
I'm still that same arrogant and ignorant
hotheaded loudmouth
who always had to have the last word.
As if I were still fond of that version of me.

She and I are not friends.
I, too, grew tired of her bullshit
and had to leave her behind.
And every time you bring her up
or speak to me as if I were still her,
you only make me think
that I should have left you behind with her.
You clearly deserve one another.

**When you get involved with a pot-stirrer,
you don't get to be surprised or upset
when friends and family
start opting out of meals.**

Erika Hayden

It is a sickness, a sadness
that never departs.
No matter the sun or smiles,
the shadow lurks in your heart.

It casts doubt, has a biting tongue,
and suffers you in silence,
but it seems that your sickness
likes me too.
It's chosen two to torment,
to drive to the edge of despair,
of madness—
to the utter depths of loathing.

Does its hold on you lessen
the more you lash out at me?
Do you get a reprieve
if you do so unprovoked?

They say it's genetic,
but my will, I promise, will conquer it.
Be in my blood or not, he will not see it.
Will not feel it. Won't even know to look.

Whenever resolve wavers,
I remind myself. Redeem myself.
"I love my son more
than my mother hates me."
The pain she feels she needs
to inflict on me,
I will not pass on to him.
I love my child more
than my mother resents hers.

We don't have to talk about it.
We're really good at keeping quiet anyway.
If only we were as good at hiding
that something is wrong
as we are at hiding our hurt.

If only we cared as much
about sparing the other wounds
as we do about hiding ours.

Maybe if we opened them up
and showed each other
precisely what makes us bleed,
perhaps we might heal.

Does your past blind you to your present?
In your haste
to be everything you needed them to be,
—everything they weren't—
did you forget that maybe, MAYBE
it might be exactly what someone
would someday *need* you to be?
Did your efforts to be more
than they ever were for you,
end up being exactly what had others
turning away?

Why did you decide to base who you are
on how you thought
someone else should have been?

When you look at them now
and think about how much better they'd be
if they'd just been what you'd thought
they should have been the whole time,
does that feeling of being right . . . feel wrong?
Because it should.

You cannot reverse-engineer perfection
from what you view to be broken.

You spin stories
like a spider does a web.
Pulling people in and
then ensnaring them.

They're enchanted at first,
believing you're the same.
Friends.
But for you, they've always been prey.
In your beautiful web of lies, they have
always been captives more than companions.

They were always meant to be consumed,
fodder for your own gain.
Be it soul food, encouragement, or a workhorse;
their fate was always the same:
To serve you.

They weren't the only ones fooled.
You enchant yourself too,
deluding yourself with the belief
that they willingly sacrificed themselves for you.
What chance did they have?
You made their options clear:
Sacrifice yourself to me, privately,
or be destroyed,
here on my beautiful web
for all to see.

That's your secret to success.
Your most valuable skill.
You know how to pick the good ones;

the loyal, generous, and tenderhearted.
They've the most to give
and do so willingly.
For a time, at least
afterwards . . . ?
Well, it's the beautiful souls
that break the prettiest.

If anger is an enemy,
what does that make you
for awakening such a beast in me?

And what does that make me
for allowing it?
For not turning you away.

And, my goodness, why
do I carry it with me
instead of the nonchalance
that you carry with you?

That smile of yours,
proud and triumphant.
"That'll teach you."

Except it won't.

Humiliation doesn't aid in learning.
It doesn't increase retention.
It breeds resentment
and self-loathing.

The only thing *it* taught me
was that I can never trust you.
Congratulations.

Erika Hayden

You slither among the corpses
of all those you poisoned,
feeding upon their weaknesses
in hopes it will make you strong.

Eyes shining with envy and loathing,
you sit in the shadows,
seething over how your venom cannot reach
those who live in the light.

The thing about demons
is that they aren't just cruel,
they're seductive.

They bed you in the darkness,
convincing you the light kills,
and that the greatest dangers
lie not with them
but outside
where the light exposes you
for exactly who you are.

They whisper
in your happiest hours
and scream in your loneliest
all your shortcomings, your flaws,
your have-nots, can-nots, and wont-bes.

They woo you
into believing their lies as truths,
into thinking that your trials are earned,
and accepting the present
as eternal.

Erika Hayden

I'll set fire to this place
and watch the embers ascend,
forming constellations
I'll guide myself by,
a trail I'll blaze
to a brighter future. . .
leaving true darkness behind.

Ghosts in the Moonlight

I only fear the dark
when my thoughts are darker.

When the world around me is too silent,
and my thoughts much too loud.
When the shadows slither closer
and bleed into my skin,
converging with the desolation within
that has stripped me bare and left me to ruin.

When I need light more than breath
to remind me that the void hasn't
swallowed me completely,
to show me where to look
to keep from sinking further.
Somewhere to claw my way towards,
where the demons fear to follow.
A place I'm too afraid to taint
with more than just a visit.

I only fear the dark
in those moments when I realize
that it is exactly where I belong.

Erika Hayden

The silence calls me, truly.
Though, truly, it's not silence
echoing my thoughts and fears,
threatening me with violence.

The shadows creep along the walls.
Contempt and malice extending,
reminding me that I'm a fraud.
They all know I'm pretending.

Why does the blackness of a starless
night seem to swallow you whole?
Overcoming us with feelings
of abandonment and inadequacy.
The illusion of solitude.
Willing you to curl in on yourself
as your demons burst forth.
Shrinking. Withering. Fading.
Is it fear that causes this withdrawal,
or exhaustion?

What if it is the sheer volume
of secrets you keep locked inside
that keeps you standing tall
rather than the drive to succeed
and prove the doubters wrong?
What if the will to go on
is simply inertia, and we're
just too beat down to question it?

Why do we feel safest
examining our flaws in the dark,
where they can destroy us
without witness or interference?
Why do we give them this power?
We create these monsters.
Train them. Educate them
on all our weaknesses and
the most efficient ways to
bring about our undoing,
then let them issue our fate.
A jury of adversaries rather than peers.
And the same verdict. Every time.
With harsh sentences they've convinced
us we've earned.

Erika Hayden

Why do we feel pain, sorrow,
and anger more deeply
than joy, hope, and satisfaction?
How does rain amplify these feelings
and make us feel as if *then*
is the only safe time to cry?

Why do we bury such feelings
inside ourselves, yet somehow
still let them burden our shoulders?

How is silence so loud
and emptiness so suffocating?
How are words left unsaid more painful
than those said in anger?
And why are the words
that our souls scream loudest
the hardest ones to say?
Somehow, the discomfort
of holding them in
always seems preferable
than the pain associated with
whatever response they'd garner.

Why is it only when we are broken
that we realize and understand
what is missing from the whole?
Despair provides clarity,
but the darkness prevents us
from dropping breadcrumbs
to follow later when the light returns.

Why is it,
that when the darkness consumes us,
we stop looking for the sunrise?

Kindness is King,
but Truth is Queen,
and just as in chess,
the King has no power
in the Queen's absence.

Erika Hayden

**Just beyond fear
lies greatness,
for all those brave enough
to reach out and take it.**

What if we aren't eroding?
Wearing ourselves away
little by little
until only a few pieces
of what we once were
remain.

What if, perhaps,
we're excavating
our true selves?
Tearing down old facades,
brushing aside
the falsehoods we followed,
the insecurities we guarded,
and the restrictions we believed.
Uncovering our genuine selves.

Would we be kinder
to ourselves then
when we look down
at our dirty hands
and skinned knees?

What braver thing
than to become
who you are meant to be?
For to do so,
one must let go
of all they once were.

Erika Hayden

**A conversation
both casual and profound
frees us our burdens.**

It's the late nights,
curled up and cozy
in dimly lit corners,
talking of days gone by,
the way we were, the whys.

The dreams we had then
versus the ones we have now,
and the secret ones
we've had all this time.

It's the tales we tell
of the scars that shaped us,
the lessons learned,
and triumphs earned.
The what-ifs and why-didn't-Is.

The vastly different paths
we each took that somehow
brought us both here.

It's knowing there'll be
many more nights like this
that make these
long absences bearable
and brings me solace.

**Understand these words:
It never hurt to love you.
It made my life full.**

You're always there to listen
to the thoughts and feelings
that seem too big for me
to hold on my own . . .
both to carry and to sit with.

I lay my head in your lap
and confess all my faults and errs
to nonjudgmental ears, wondering
how I earned such patience and compassion.
The only safe place I've ever found
with a population of more than just myself.

Free of ulterior motives and questions,
utterly absent of lectures and advice.
A refuge to unload the burdens
born of bravery, obstinance, and ambition
but made heavier by doubt and expectation.
A respite between battles,
both internal and external.
A treasure all seek, and a lottery
too few in this life win.

Silence between us,
devoid of expectation.
Companionable.

You always seem to know
Just what to say.
Always know which words
get stuck in my throat.
What feelings
I'm not brave enough to voice.

Hope is a flower,
the first to brave winter's chill
and inspire change.

Erika Hayden

Erika Hayden

It's easy to forget how lonely I am
during the waking hours . . .
until I come home. Head bursting
from too many thoughts and insecurities,
I try to silence them
with wine and mindless television.

My heart concedes its defeat
as I cuddle up to a pillow and lie to myself
when I think it's comparable to a man.

Eyes squeezing tightly
as everything I think and feel
crowds the room around me,
amplifying the emptiness, echoing inside me.
Smothering the fire within.
Crushing the heart I hide away,
the cracked and broken one
too stubborn to stop beating
despite the beatings it keeps taking.

And no comfort to be found
in the fact that the loneliness
is all I have now to keep me company.

**To live life genuinely,
you must share
all that is inside
with all who are outside.**

Move with purpose,
no matter how broken
and uneven the path before you.

When your heart wavers
and uncertainty seizes your breath.
When your courage feels small,
and your resolve timid and full of doubt.

Let purpose lend
mettle to your conviction,
grit to your perseverance,
and longevity to your strength of will
as it illuminates the dark roads,
pushing us forward towards the unknown.
Giving worth to adversity and triumphs.

And if you find that it eludes you,
move first with intention . . .
Purpose is known for nipping at its heels.

I am more than a collection
of traits, opinions, and behaviors.
More than a series of events
that make up my past.
More than the dreams and drive
creating my future—
presently and otherwise.

Ever-growing and evolving,
forever searching and finding.
Always aiming and striving
to define and recognize me.

Erika Hayden

Know that your own awakening
will inspire others
who, too, want to live
a genuine and authentic life.
Be supportive and encouraging.
Use caution, though,
for those who follow your direct path
are not brave enough to forge their own.
Their goal isn't to seek their own
happiness and fulfillment,
but to siphon off yours.

No matter their intentions
or level of consciousness,
they are parasites,
incapable of their own growth.
Do not burden yourself with the guilt
of outpacing them.

We are like pinnacles near the sea.
Some bravely standing out
amidst the ocean waves,
open, engaging, and carefree,
embracing all the world has to give.
Noted in photography and lore,
revered for their beauty and majesty.
For the spirit they embody and inspire.

Others
stay closer to the shore,
lasting longer than
their bolder, more captivating brethren.
Safe from the pounding waves, and pressure.
At least for a while. . . But over time,
they see and feel more,
then they too transform.
Wearing down those walls,
revealing a living sculpture.
A treasure.
A sight to behold.

They were always a masterpiece,
but by the time they believed
and thought themselves beautiful,
confident, and worthwhile,
the others they longed to be like were gone,
and they finds themselves, alone . . . still.

Erika Hayden

I've always been here
by your side, supporting you
I always will be.

Erika Hayden

I'm unfolding
after a lifetime of holding myself
tightly together, strong and proud.
Of shielding the novel features,
protecting parts most tender,
and guarding hidden treasures.
The vulnerability of my defenses
now exposed . . . and permeable.

I'm unfolding.
These walls worn thin from within,
from the desperation of wanting
to be seen and heard—perhaps
even valued. Impossible when concealed.
For if unknown and undiscovered,
who's to give value? To marvel,
or to covet? To seek to obtain?
My fortress made obsolete
by my skewed preservation instinct.

I'm unfolding
before my efforts devalue
all the facets of myself
I fought so hard to protect.
Before all that is without and within
are in ruins. A travesty.
A cautionary tale
mapped out and toured
as all I held dear is stepped over
by those who see such artifacts and think:
"I would have loved this.
How I wish I could have beheld this
in its prime—pristine and radiant.
I'm jealous of all who did."
Not knowing that none were ever allowed.

So, I'm unfolding.

What's to say it's not enough
for one person to find meaning
in a single poem written here?
Who's to say that said meaning
is fleeting or anything less
than profound?

If we're all influenced by
—and thus influence—
everything we encounter,
how certain can we be
that those effects don't create ripples
and move through us? Or *with* us?

Is it not entirely possible, then,
that an assemblage of words
read at just the right, or wrong, time
could dramatically change the
seemingly insignificant life
of an unsure soul
and put them on track to
tremendously impact the lives of
everyone else who reads that same poem
and finds it remarkably unremarkable?

**Remember, my dear,
love transcends. Envy erodes.
That's the difference.**

Dear helicopter parents:
Remember,
you are a safety net
meant to catch them if they fall.
You're not supposed to be
wrapped around them. . .
like a straitjacket.

With the diagnosis comes the stagger.
The dazed confusion, disorientation. The denial.
The . . . *what just happened?*
And *how did this happen?*

The *what do I do now?* comes later.
You might wonder if it's all over before
you've even had a chance to fight back.
You try to keep your feet. You stumble.
Maybe you fall.
But you get back up . . . you WILL get back up.
Because you're a warrior,
and now's the time to prove it.
Shake the doubts out of your head
and square back up.

Now, you can form a plan.
Now, you can face your opponent.
Make cancer fear for its life
'cause yours isn't over yet.
Not by a long shot.

You say, "I'm a lover, not a fighter."
Except this time, you're both. You have to be.
But it's because of love that you will fight.

You'll lace up those boots because you love
yourself too much to turn away from a challenge.
You'll don those gloves
because you love your family too much
to let *this* decide the future for them.
You'll bite down on the mouthguard
and you'll enter that ring
because . . . *fuck cancer* if it thinks it's going to win.

The doctors told you the stage,
and the stage may be set,
but this is no curtain call.
Not yet it's not.
Cancer isn't undefeated.
It isn't a death sentence.
And you're about to show it
just how much life and fight you've got left.

We never want to leave loved ones
to face Goliath on their own.
We want to be by their sides, swords drawn,
ready to charge in beside them.
We can't bear the thought of stepping aside
and letting them enter the arena solo.
That's not what friends do.
Not what family does . . .
every other time but this one.

Cancer is a solo battle.
It is between the patient and the masses.
The weapons they choose to use
are theirs alone.
What you would use doesn't matter.
Your battle plan doesn't matter.
All that matters is unconditional support.

Keep your, "If it were me, I'd . . ."
and your, "I don't understand why. . ."
They don't matter either.
All you need to say is, "I'm here if you need me."
They don't want your opinions;
they don't want to hear about someone else's fight
because that's not what's trying to kill them.
All they want is you in their corner.
So shut your mouth and show up.

Erika Hayden

**All the light
we cannot see
shines brightest
within us
when we let ourselves
breathe.**

In a handful of years
we became intimate,
Death and me.

From estranged to bi-yearly visits.
Then every few months.
Mourning clothes
to mark the change of seasons,
and another morning with heavy hearts,
bursting apart with too many memories.
Or aching from far too few.
Our busy lives slackening the thread
that connected us.

Death moved through this family
like an enraged bull through a garden,
tearing some up from the roots,
trampling others.
Flowers strewn across the ravaged and lost.

We saw its many faces,
the rich and varied life Death leads.
Old age, heart failure, cancer, suicide,
kidney failure, cancer again, car accident,
heart attack, Crohn's . . .
A reminder that Death isn't choosy in its choices.
And likes surprises.
The young mother, the widower.
The treasured son in a family of daughters.
The saint who ran a soup kitchen for decades.
The thirty-five-year-old father, the "lucky" one.
The matriarch and cornerstone of the family
of several families—including mine.

Erika Hayden

For too long now,
Death has fallen like a blanket over us.
But I'm ready now. To stop mourning.
It's time to throw off the blanket of Death
and get up. Time for Life and me
to become even more intimate.

They say life is divided
into "before" and "after"
when you get the diagnosis.
When life suddenly has two dates.

For me, the divide isn't my own
diagnosis but my mother's.
It was August. Three months later,
a cousin got hers too—she was my age.

By the next August, my cousin was gone.
By February, my mother too.
Eighteen months was her fight.
And eighteen months after that, I started mine.

I was in for something else. Something simple.
Concerned looks turned into test requests.
It was August. Three months later
and I'm halfway through chemo.
I have to stay strong; the road gets harder.

For me, the divide isn't my own
diagnosis. But for him, it is.
He already lost his father, suddenly.
And now he could be an orphan—in slow motion.

Every day with him has been a gift
since the day he was born.
It was August. Three months later,
I was still scared. I still wasn't ready.
I didn't know what I was doing,
but I was doing it.

Erika Hayden

Now, every day, I make a gift for him
to cushion the blow of what's to come:
radiation, surgery, a mother he won't recognize.
I have to stay strong; the road gets harder.

By August, the cancer should be gone.
By February actually. The breasts too.
I'm still scared. I'm still not ready.
I still don't know what I'm doing,
but I'm doing it. For him.
I'm doing it, and I'm going to win.

neon bubbles float in a florescent forest
a child dancing wildly around me
his laughter joining the chorus
of wind, of frogs and crickets

remember this, my love,
these moments
when it was just you and me
out having adventures
wild and free

Ghosts in the Moonlight

Erika Hayden

**You sleep peacefully,
unaware of the burdens
I will always bear.**

Ghosts in the Moonlight

That moment when your heart bursts with love
as the sun creeps in through the window,
and he rolls over.
He blinks the sleep from his eyes
and looks at you,
then gifts you his biggest, most joyous smile.
The same one he flashed you years ago
when all he knew how to do was that. And cry.

It's the grin that lets you know
he's happier to see you
than to return to those sweetest of dreams.
And that any nightmares that dared to enter
his head now cower before you.
Those bright eyes tug on the tether connecting
your heart to his.
That, "Good morning, Mommy,"
conveying pure contentment and love.
And, perhaps, mischievous excitement
for the day ahead.

That same moment breaks your heart, though,
because he's flirting with double digits
and is already so tall.
And you know it won't be long
until he's too old to lie with you.
Too old to want to cuddle and have tickle fights.
Too old to want to protect you from *your* nightmares . . .
Nightmares of the coming day when
he reaches the age of not needing you.
Of not being able—or maybe willing—to reveal
that indeed he still does.

Erika Hayden

It's only a matter of time until a new kind of loneliness
creeps in like the sun but far more devastating,
and your once bursting heart
is on the verge of crumbling.
Days when the scene before you
will be so distant, you'll wonder
how the years managed to blaze by so fast
and question if your sweet boy
recalls them as fondly as you.

I never meant for you
to feel any of my failures.
Not due to any shame I felt
but because your two little legs
should never bear such burdens.

I know it's selfish,
and I'm sorry.
I don't know how *not* to be, though.
Not right now.
Not when I'm acutely aware
of all that I'll be missing.

It's almost time,
and I've hardly worked out
how I'm supposed to feel.

I'm terrified
of the darkness I know will take me.
Of the bone-deep cold that will follow.
The silence.
I've never feared it before now—
I craved it even—But I take back
every time I begged for it,
especially knowing that
I'll never again hear that sweet laugh
spilling from behind that mischievous smile.
The grief of that knowledge is breaking me.

I want more time.
Here, with you.
I sincerely regret every day
I wished had gone by faster.
I'm furious with myself for that.
All those hours thrown away.
Those unappreciated moments
wasted in the name of fatigue.

I need more time.

Erika Hayden

Just one more minute to memorize
the exact color of your eyes.
The shade and shape of your lips.
The precise angle
of that lopsided grin—
the one you try to hide.
And the creamy complexion of your face
with those freckles you got from me.
Forgive me for staring,
but it's the last time I'll ever see them.

Goddammit.
Just give me a few moments more
to hold you, my sweet, beautiful child.
I don't want to leave you.
How am I to be without you?
You've always been my whole world.

How can I possibly stomach
the idea of leaving you alone?
I'm supposed to always be here for you.
It's my job to protect you,
to spare you pain,
and soothe your fears.
I failed you,
and I won't ever forgive myself for it.
I'm sorry. I'm so sorry, honey.
Please, forgive me.

I'm here now, sweetheart.
We're together.
We always will be.
Don't be afraid.
But please,
please
don't leave me.

Don't let my death jade you.
Don't let it turn you cold and hard.
That is not who you are.
You are love personified.
You always have been.

All the things you loved and will miss about me,
were birthed by you.
All the joy and laughter,
the long mornings in bed,
and the late-night movie nights.
The impromptu adventures,
the mind-wanderings and ponderings . . .
All of that, all of *me* . . . is you.

I was who I was because of you.
I did not mold you into who you are now.
You molded *me*.
Parents become who their children need vthem to be.
You, above all things, needed love.
To replenish all the love you so freely gave
to everyone you met.

I was only me because I loved you.
So, when you miss me most,
love yourself the way I loved you.
With everything I was.
Completely. Shamelessly. Recklessly.

Weep not for me,
because I am free.
The way we both need me to be.
To watch over you selflessly
so the love you had for me
can be turned inwardly.

Weep not, for I did not lose this fight.
I did not "go softly, into that good night."
Breathe and believe that you will be all right,
for our spirits have fused, bestowing you my might.
And though I may be gone from your sight,
you'll find me, always, in dawning light.

Weep not that you've no one to hold.
Know that I'm still here, shielding you from cold
and the weariness creeping into your soul.
Arise, love. Strong, renewed, invigored, and bold.
For I reside now within you, as fate has foretold.

Afterword

A note about discomfort:
These poems, those that are true, are MY truth . . . and were not written in the most comforting and palatable way. Quite the opposite, actually. And intentionally. They were also written when seized by emotion—emotion that by its very nature amplifies and sensationalizes itself. Emotion that demands to be felt and heard.

There is a LOT of truth within these pages. Things I wasn't comfortable putting down, and truths many won't be comfortable soaking up . . . but voicing them is a form of kindness. To me, to others not ready to voice or even acknowledge their own truths, and to those who inflict wounds without care or cause because they actively ignore their own. I will always be someone willing to do the uncomfortable to make others comfortable. Willing to bear the burden. This burden frees others . . . and me.

I hope parading my ghosts in the moonlight helps free *you*—even if temporarily—from yours.

A note for readers of the familiar kind:
You may think you know whom certain pieces are about. And for some, you may be correct. But before you commit to your assumptions, remind yourselves that I am an empath and also a writer of both truth AND fiction. I channeled some of these poems from others—both real people and characters. While there's no *right* way to read poetry, there *are* wrong ways . . . and as a detective trying to identify a suspect is one of them. If you find yourselves trying to uncover an identity as you read these pages instead of feeling what the words were intended to evoke, then put the book down and try again later.

Also, keep in mind that we know different versions of the same people . . . and those versions don't necessarily look anything alike. It's entirely possible that we wouldn't even recognize the one the other knows.

And that's okay.

About the Author

Like many born and raised in the Midwest, Erika Hayden strives to be that perfect mix of spirited and endearing. She enjoys challenging people's perceptions and expectation using both tried and true methods as well as those that are novel and shocking. Her most notable achievements in this field include: disliking chocolate, caramel, and everything pumpkin spice, preferring full contact sports to shopping, making even the most innocent and mundane sentences into double entendres/ puns/ innuendos/ euphemisms (or a delightful orgy of all those), having complete conversations using movie and TV quotes, and being a foul-mouthed intellectual.

Erika stunned the world by giving birth to a child that likes to talk even more than she does (usually while ricocheting of the walls) and who, like his mother, enjoys "enticing and confusing" others—his words. One would presume this leaves her little time or energy to do much else, and they would be absolutely correct. For that reason, should you know of a man both eager and capable of handling such a treasure of a woman, please send him to the Mitten. Serious inquiries only. Must be able to speak/text in complete sentences. No baseball, Ohio State, or Alabama fans (that should weed out most of the weird ones).

Should the mood strike you, you can find her online or wandering the woods (for best results, bait your traps with tacos or sushi).

Erika Hayden